Heritage
of the Lord

The blessings of the Lord be upon you

Toyin

Heritage
of the Lord

Prayers and Confessions For Your Children

Silverspring, Maryland
Nov 2012

TOYIN FASOSIN

© 2011 by Toyin Fasosin. All rights reserved.

WinePress Publishing (PO Box 428, Enumclaw, WA 98022) functions only as book publisher. As such, the ultimate design, content, editorial accuracy, and views expressed or implied in this work are those of the author.

No part of this publication may be reproduced, stored in a retrieval system, or transmitted in any way by any means—electronic, mechanical, photocopy, recording, or otherwise—without the prior permission of the copyright holder, except as provided by USA copyright law.

Unless otherwise noted, all Scriptures are taken from the *King James Version* of the Bible.

ISBN 13: 978-1-4141-2091-1
ISBN 10: 1-4141-2091-5
Library of Congress Catalog Card Number: 2011927812

I dedicate this book:

> To my loving Father and God, who loves me so much that He gave His best to redeem me.
>
> To Jesus, for loving me enough to pay the ultimate sacrifice. There is truly no love greater than this.
>
> To the Holy Spirit, for constantly showing me the way chosen for me. You are the best Teacher and Guide.

Contents

Acknowledgments.........................ix

Foreword................................xi

1. Heritage of the Lord 1
2. Coming to Christ 5
3. Returning to the Father's House 9
4. Seeking God's Kingdom 13
5. Growing Up Spiritually..................15
6. Fulfilling Purpose 19
7. Having a Sound Mind 23
8. The Place of Honor 29
9. Exhibiting Brotherly Love................33
10. Building Godly Connections.............37
11. Burgeoning Sexuality 41

12. Leaving and Cleaving 47
13. Loving to Learn. 51
14. Walking in Healing and
     Wholeness. 55
15. Taking Proper Care of the Body 59
16. Living in the Place of Protection. 63
17. Giving Thanks. 67

Prayer of Salvation 71

Acknowledgments

WITH SPECIAL THANKS:

To my husband and best friend, Bimbola, who faithfully supports me in all I do.

To my lovely children—Tomisin, Teniayo, and Tomiwa— for the joy you bring and for causing me to pray.

To my parents, Professor and Mrs. J. B. Akingba, for teaching me to pray.

To my pastor, Ghandi Olaoye, for inspiring me to see the invisible and believe the impossible.

Foreword

*H*ERITAGE OF THE Lord is a must-have for parents everywhere. Our children are the most valued parts of our lives, and as Christians, our utmost desire is that they will believe in Christ even as we have believed. As parents, we are constantly concerned about the future of our children. We invest so much in them to ensure they have the things they need to succeed in life. What better gift can we give them than a life dedicated to constant prayers for and over their lives? Then we can spiritually lift them into the presence of God daily so that when they are eventually grown, we can witness how God shaped them into the people He designed them to be.

Because of the uniqueness of each child, we parents cannot afford to just pray "one size fits all" prayers for them or make generic confessions over their lives. Therefore, this book guides you to specific prayers that will more than likely be applicable to the prayers and biblical confessions you would want to make over your child. The various areas of focus highlighted in the book address different stages of a child's growth and spiritual development, even choices the child will need to make as he or she grows all the way from infancy to adulthood.

Toyin Fasosin has put together a keepsake for every parent, grandparent, leader, mentor, and anyone who has a heart to pray the younger generation into their God-given destinies. It is a book that will yield many dividends; the children who grow up under such auspices will most undoubtedly repeat the same prayers for their own children in time to come. This book is a priceless treasure, and I highly recommend it!

Pastor Ghandi Olaoye
Senior Pastor
Redeemed Christian Church of God
Jesus House, DC
Silver Spring, Maryland

Chapter 1

Heritage of the Lord

LO, CHILDREN ARE an heritage of the Lord: and the fruit of the womb is his reward. As arrows are in the hand of a mighty man; so are children of the youth. Happy is the man that hath his quiver full of them: they shall not be ashamed, but they shall speak with the enemies in the gate" (Ps. 127:3–5).

The word[1] *heritage* means "legacy, birthright, something transmitted or acquired from a predecessor, something transmitted as a result of one's natural situation or birth, a right, privilege, or possession to which a person is entitled by birth."

---

[1] "Heritage." Merriam-Webster® Online Dictionary. 2011 http://www.merriam-webster.com (18 May, 2011)

Heritage of the Lord

Children are a right or possession to which every believer in Christ Jesus is entitled. Malachi 2:15 states that the Lord makes a man and his wife one, because He desires godly children from them. God desires us to raise our children in His ways, training them by teaching and example and helping them discover and prepare for the work He has assigned to them.

God has an individual plan for each of our children; even identical twins do not share the same plan. He has established an apportioned race they must run, an assignment they must complete. They will achieve their greatest fulfillment and find their deepest joy only by pursuing what they were created for.

Our role as parents is to help our children discover, develop, and use the gifts within them. We need to receive wisdom from God on the way He has already chosen for them, and on our role of ensuring that they find and remain on it.

Psalm 127:3–5 likens children to arrows in the hand of a warrior. Warriors don't just release their arrows, hoping and praying they will hit the mark. They carefully take aim until they are certain an arrow is properly aligned before they release it. Warriors spend more time taking aim than releasing the arrow.

We must be very purposeful in raising our children; it is our responsibility to train them in the way of the Lord and to direct them toward their assignment.

Heritage of the Lord

My husband and I have three wonderful children, and even at these stages of their lives, I can identify specific strengths and different behaviors. I must structure my teaching and discipline based on each child's personality; one size does not fit all. The ground rules are the same, but implementation differs.

Heritage of the Lord came about from Scriptures I have used in prayer and confession for my children over the years. For a while I searched for a book for parents that contains both prayers and confessions, but only found either one or the other.

My hope is that this book will encourage a start to a well-structured and fulfilling life of prayers and confessions over your children. Declare these prayers and confessions over them every day. In critical situations, repeat the confessions as often as possible, especially if your mind is in turmoil and fear tries to overwhelm you.

I pray you will see the fruit of your labor over your children and rejoice in raising the heritage of the Lord.

Chapter 2

Coming to Christ

GOD DESIRES THAT all men and women would be saved and come to the knowledge of the truth (1 Tim. 2:4). It is our responsibility as parents to raise godly children (Mal. 2:15). We prepare our children to receive Jesus as their Lord and Savior by precept and example. The Enemy, on the other hand, seeks to blind the minds of our children so they will not believe and so "the light of the glorious gospel of Christ…[will not] shine unto them" (2 Cor. 4:4).

We must pray to remove the blinders from their minds and to loose them from bondage so they can receive Jesus. We must continue praying for them after they are born again so Christ may be fully formed in them (Gal. 4:19)

Heritage of the Lord

Prayer

Dear Father, thank You for (child's name). I know You don't desire the death of any sinner but that all should come to know the truth.

I pray that (child's name) will come to know You. I ask for the removal of whatever the Devil has used to blind his or her mind. I ask for the light of the glorious gospel to shine unto (child's name).
—2 Cor. 4:4

I ask that (child's name) might confess Jesus as Lord and believe in his or her heart that You have raised Him from the dead.
—Rom. 10:9

I ask that (child's name) will receive the baptism of the Holy Spirit with the evidence of speaking in tongues and that (child's name) might be filled with the knowledge of Your will in all wisdom and spiritual understanding.
—Col. 1:9

I intercede on (child's name)'s behalf until Christ is fully formed in him or her.
—Gal. 4:19

Thank You, Father, that Your hand is upon (child's name) to deliver and to save. Thank You that (child's name) will serve You all the days of his or her life.

Coming to Christ

Confessions

As for me and my house, we will serve the Lord.
—Josh. 24:15

(Child's name) listens to me as I teach him or her the fear of the Lord.
—Ps. 34:11

(Child's name) is taken away from the mighty and delivered from the terrible. The Lord fights with him who fights with me and saves (child's name).
—Isa. 49:25

(Child's name) loves the Lord, his or her God, with all his or her heart, soul, mind, and strength.
—Mark 12:30

(Child's name) is a child of light and of the day; he or she is neither of the night nor of darkness.
—1 Thess. 5:5

(Child's name) keeps himself or herself from idols. Amen.
—1 John 5:21

Chapter 3

Returning to the Father's House

THE HEART OF God is that of a loving father, as revealed in the story of the younger son who returned home after wasting his inheritance on a wild lifestyle (Luke 15:11–32). The father saw him from a distance, had compassion on him, and ran to kiss him. What grace! What love! This is the true nature of God.

God is ever ready to receive anyone who returns to Him. "He is faithful and just to forgive…and… cleanse us from all unrighteousness" (1 John 1:9).

Prayer

> Dear Father, thank You for love that will not let us go. Thank You for restoration and deliverance. I pray that (child's name) will return to You. I ask that (child's name) will confess his or her sins

to You. I thank You for being faithful and just to forgive and to cleanse (child's name) from all unrighteousness.
—1 John 1:9

Lord, help (child's name) to be quick to repent, to humble himself or herself before You and receive Your mercy and grace. I ask that (child's name) will not live in guilt or condemnation but will believe in and receive Your love and forgiveness as well as the restoration of fellowship with You.

Thank You, Lord, that there is no condemnation for (child's name) because he or she now walks according to Your Word and the leading of Your Spirit, not according to his or her senses.

Confessions

The Lord sends His hand from above to deliver (child's name) out of great waters, from the hand of strange children. The Lord delivers (child's name) from the hand of strange children, whose mouths speak vanity and whose right hand is a right hand of falsehood.
—Ps. 144:7, 11

I arise and cry out in the night: in the beginning of the watches I pour out my heart like water before the face of the Lord: I lift up my hands toward Him for the life of (child's name).
—Lam. 2:19

I stop weeping, for my work concerning (child's name) shall be rewarded, and he or she shall come again from the land of the enemy. The Lord said there is hope in my end, that (child's name) shall come again to his or her own border.

—Jer. 31:16–17

The Lord is faithful and just to forgive (child's name)'s sins and to cleanse him or her from all unrighteousness.

—1 John 1:9

Chapter 4

Seeking God's Kingdom

"BUT SEEK YE first the kingdom of God, and his righteousness; and all these things shall be added unto you" (Matt. 6:33).

God's number-one priority in the earth is the advancement of His kingdom. He has left the church here to extend the reach of His influence and to enforce His will on earth as it is in heaven.

We must teach our children to put God first in everything they do. As they do so, He has promised to meet all their physical needs, including food, shelter, and clothing.

Prayer

Father, I thank You for making (child's name) Your son or daughter. I thank You for loving (child's name) and preparing the best life possible for him or her.

Give (child's name) wisdom on how to seek first Your kingdom and equip him or her to excel in Your service.

May (child's name) not lose focus and begin to pursue after things, but rather obey orders as a good soldier of Christ.

Confessions

(Child's name)'s first priority is seeking the kingdom of God and His righteousness; therefore, God gives him or her all material things.
—Matt. 6:33

(Child's name)'s primary goal is to please God and do His will; he or she will not lose focus.
—2 Tim. 2:4

(Child's name) is willing and obedient and enjoys the best life has to offer.
—Isa. 1:19

God has given (child's name) knowledge of the secrets of the kingdom.
—Matt. 13:11

(Child's name) endures hardness as a highly disciplined soldier of Christ Jesus.
—2 Tim. 2:3

Chapter 5

Growing Up Spiritually

SALVATION OR THE new birth is instantaneous, but growth is progressive. The Bible recognizes three stages of spiritual growth: babe (1 Cor. 3:1–3; Heb. 5:12–13), child (1 Cor. 13:11), and full age (Heb. 5:14).

We need to earnestly pray for our children that they will always hunger to increase in their relationship with God and will never feel they have arrived but will "press toward the mark" of becoming like Jesus (Phil. 3:13–15).

Prayer

> Lord, I praise You for all You are doing in (child's name)'s life. Thank You for Your commitment to his or her growth and development. Thank You for providing all the tools required to

ensure (child's name)'s success in every endeavor of life.

Father, I ask that (child's name) will hunger and thirst for You all the days of his or her life and that (child's name) will grow in grace and be an example of a believer in thought, word, and deed.

Let (child's name)'s life be a fragrance unto You.

Confessions

(Child's name) lays aside all malice, all deception, all inconsistencies or falseness, all envy, and all evil speaking. He or she desires the sincere milk of the word and grows.

—1 Peter 2:1–2

(Child's name) grows up in Christ in all things by speaking the truth in love.

—Eph. 4:15

(Child's name) grows in grace and in the knowledge of our Lord and Savior Jesus Christ.
—2 Peter 3:18

(Child's name) grows in love, knowledge, and understanding.

—Phil. 1:9

Growing Up Spiritually

(Child's name) excels in everything: in faith, speaking, knowledge, diligence, love, and giving.
—2 Cor. 8:7

God's love fills (child's name)'s heart by the Holy Spirit.
—Rom. 5:5

(Child's name) increases and develops in love, joy, peace, longsuffering, kindness, goodness, faithfulness, gentleness, and self-control.
—Gal. 5:22–23

Chapter 6

Fulfilling Purpose

WE ARE HERE on assignment. Each of us is God's masterpiece, created in Christ Jesus to do a work He prepared ahead of time (Eph. 1:10).

God has not called everyone into full-time or the five-fold ministry—apostle, prophet, evangelist, pastor, and teacher (Eph. 4:11). But we all have a role to play in the body of Christ and the world.

We need to ask God to reveal to us the assignments and abilities He has for each child so we can train our children to live in line with them (Prov. 22:6).

God's gifts and calling are irrevocable, and He will judge our children based on their compliance to His plans for them.

Prayer

Dear Father, thank You for giving (child's name) a future and a hope.
—Jer. 29:11

I pray You will reveal to me (child's name)'s assignment and the abilities and talents You have placed in him or her to fulfill it. Show me how to help (child's name) discover, develop, and maximize every potential.

I ask that he or she will walk worthy of the assignment You have given and not compare it to or long for another's.
—Eph. 4:1

May (child's name) finish strong and complete the assignment.

Confessions

(Child's name) is God's masterpiece, created in Christ Jesus to do a work He prepared ahead of time.
—Eph. 2:10

(Child's name) is faithful to the call and honest both in private and public.
—1 Cor. 4:2; 2 Cor. 8:21

Fulfilling Purpose

(Child's name) is diligent to fulfill his or her assignment.
—Col. 4:17

(Child's name) is diligent to the end and through faith and patience inherits the promises.
—Heb. 6:11–12

(Child's name) lays aside every distraction and sinful habit and runs with endurance the race set before him or her, focusing on Jesus, the source and finisher of his or her faith.
—Heb. 12:1–2

(Child's name) is diligent in everything he or she does, wholeheartedly serving the Lord.
—Rom. 12:11

Chapter 7

Having a Sound Mind

THE MIND IS the battlefield, and the enemy is out to gain control of our children's minds. He does so by trying to infiltrate their minds with negative thoughts and imaginations through what they see and hear.

As parents, we have the authority to control what our young children watch, read, and listen to. We can also monitor where they go or who has access to them. As they grow older, they are no longer under our constant supervision, but we can still pray for them to have sound minds.

As believers, the weapons we fight with are not physical but mighty through God to pull down strongholds (mindsets), to cast down imaginations and every argument that sets itself against the knowledge of God, and to capture every thought and make it obey Christ (2 Cor. 10:3–5).

Our children need not inherit any emotional or mental imbalance. Neither do they need to live in fear, depression, and turmoil, nor experience anxiety attacks.

We must continue to encourage our children to read, watch, listen to, and act on the Word at all times so they will prosper and succeed in everything they do (Josh. 1:8).

Prayer

Dear Father, thank You for giving (child's name) a spirit of power, love, and a sound mind. I appreciate the fact that Jesus's sacrifice also provides peace for him or her.

Lord, cause (child's name) to realize that You are that perfect love that removes all fear. I ask that (child's name) will guard his or her heart and mind through what he or she sees, hears, reads, listens to, and fellowships with.

I ask that (child's name)'s mind will be clear and alert at all times and that (child's name) will suffer neither disorientation nor panic attacks.

Christ has redeemed him or her from the curse of the law, which includes all manner of sickness and disease; therefore, I declare that (child's name) is delivered from any mental or emotional imbalance.

I pray that God will deliver (child's name) from depression, low self-esteem, and self-hatred. The joy of the Lord is (child's name)'s strength.

Having a Sound Mind

(Child's name) loves himself or herself with God's love that fills his or her heart.

Confessions

Jesus was wounded for (child's name)'s transgressions, and He was bruised for his or her iniquities; the chastisement of his or her peace was upon Him, and with His stripes (child's name) is healed.
—Isa. 53:5

The Lord has given (child's name) a spirit of power, love, and a sound mind.
—2 Tim. 1:7

(Child's name) lies down and sleeps in peace. He or she sings aloud when in bed, for the Lord makes (child's name) dwell in safety.
—Ps. 4:8; 149:5

The Lord gives (child's name) strength and blesses him or her with peace.
—Ps. 29:11

The Lord has delivered (child's name)'s soul in peace from the battle that was against him or her. He has brought (child's name) out with joy and gladness.
—Ps. 55:18; 105:43

Heritage of the Lord

(Child's name) loves God's Word; therefore, he or she has great peace, and nothing offends him or her.

—Ps. 119:165

(Child's name) goes out with joy and is led with peace.

—Isa. 55:12

For (child's name)'s shame he or she has double, and for (child's name)'s confusion he or she rejoices in his or her portion. Therefore, in (child's name)'s land he or she possesses the double and everlasting joy.

—Isa. 61:7

(Child's name) has peace in Jesus. The world has many trials and sorrows, but (child's name) rejoices because Jesus has overcome the world.

—John 16:33

The Lord keeps (child's name) in perfect peace, because he or she trusts in Him and fixes his or her thoughts on Him.

—Isa. 26:3

Having a Sound Mind

The Lord fills (child's name) with all joy and peace in believing, so he or she abounds in hope through the power of the Holy Ghost.

—Rom. 15:13

Chapter 8

The Place of Honor

MAN CRAVES RELATIONSHIPS; no one is an island. We all need to interact with others on this planet. Some relationships in life are paramount, such as parents to children, siblings, friends, and spouses. These relationships can either enhance or decrease the quality of one's life.

Honor is respect and esteem shown to others. It is composed of reverence (deep respect with love and devotion), deference (yielding to another's judgment), and preference. Honor is taught, not "caught." As parents, it is our responsibility to teach our children honor.

Honor is essential to our children's quality and length of life on the earth. God says He will honor those who honor Him and lightly esteem those who do not (1 Sam. 2:30). Honoring parents ensures a good and long life for our children (Eph. 6:1–3); therefore, we owe it to them to teach honor.

Prayer

Dear Father, teach (child's name) to truly honor You with all his or her heart, soul, thoughts, words, and actions.

Teach him or her to honor parents and other authority figures. Deliver from pride, rebellion, and stubbornness, and help him or her to be quick to grasp and obey instructions.

Lord, I pray (child's name) will honor and obey me so he or she will live long and well. Turn (child's name)'s heart to me and vice versa.

Give (child's name) a meek and quiet spirit, which is priceless before You.

Confessions

(Child's name) sings the honor of the Lord's name, making His praise glorious all day.
—Ps. 66:2; 71:8

(Child's name) honors the Lord with his or her lips as well as his or her heart, soul, and body.
—Isa. 29:13

(Child's name) is meek and gentle, giving honor to whom it is due.
—Rom. 13:7

The Place of Honor

(Child's name) obeys his or her parents in the Lord. (Child's name) honors father and mother, ensuring a long, good life.

—Eph. 6:1–3

Chapter 9

Exhibiting Brotherly Love

GOD "SETTETH THE solitary in families" (Ps. 68:6); He establishes those who are alone in families. His desire is that we be connected to each other like the threads in a tapestry. If you cut one of those threads, the entire work unravels. In the same way, a family divided against itself will fall apart (Luke 11:17).

Sibling rivalry has been a major cause of strife and dysfunction in families since the time of Cain and Abel, Jacob and Esau, and Joseph and his brothers, to name a few. We must pray for unity in our homes because that is where the Lord commands His blessing (Ps. 133:1, 3).

Prayer

Father, I pray for (child's name)'s relationship with all other family members. I pray that love and honor will reign in his or her dealings with the rest of the family.

I pull up every root of bitterness and resist every enmity within this family. May every planting the Lord has not planted be uprooted in Jesus's name.

Lord, I repair every breach and restore the paths on which to walk. I ask for restoration of every strained or broken fellowship between (child's name) and (family member's name).

May Your peace fill our hearts toward one another, and may we all live in unity, preferring one another in love.

Confessions

(Child's name) lives with (sibling's name) in unity, and the Lord releases His anointing and blessing upon their relationship.

—Ps. 133:1, 3

(Child's name) and (sibling's name) love and honor one another.

—Rom. 12:10

(Child's name) does his or her part to keep the unity of the Spirit in the bond of peace.

—Eph. 4:3

Exhibiting Brotherly Love

(Child's name) and (sibling's name) are of one mind. They live in peace, and the God of love and peace is with them.

—2 Cor. 13:11

Chapter 10

Building Godly Connections

PEER PRESSURE IS a real issue in the lives of our children; therefore, we need to pray that they will be surrounded by godly friends, role models, and mentors. We become what we behold, so it is crucial that our children have the right influences in their lives.

We must pray that they will not be "unequally yoked with unbelievers"; this relationship refers not only to marriage partners but also to close, intimate friends (2 Cor. 6:14–17).

Prayer

>Dear Father, please guide (child's name) in choosing godly friends, role models, and mentors. Help me to be a positive influence in making right relationships.

(Child's name) is here on Your assignment; help him or her to discern and cultivate the relationships that align with Your plan.

May (child's name) be attracted to godliness, not to unrighteousness.

Deliver him or her from any soul ties with undesirable elements and every unequal yoke.

Heal (child's name)'s emotions from the loss of any relationship, and bring restoration in any beneficial relationship that is strained or broken.

Confessions

(Child's name) takes no advice contrary to the Word of God. He or she neither succumbs to peer pressure to do evil nor hangs out with those who disrespect the things of God.

Instead, (child's name) loves and habitually studies the Word of God day and night.

Therefore, (child's name) is like a tree firmly planted by the rivers of water (having access to constant sustenance and nourishment), being productive in his or her season. (Child's name)'s leaf shall not fade away, and everything he or she does shall remain and develop to maturity.

—Ps. 1:1–3

Building Godly Connections

(Child's name) is an example of a believer in word, lifestyle, love, spirit, faith, and purity. He or she is a godly influence on peers and friends.
—1 Tim. 4:12

(Child's name) does not make friends with angry, impatient people; therefore, he or she neither becomes like them nor is addicted to anger.
—Prov. 22:24–25

Chapter 11

Burgeoning Sexuality

SEXUALITY IS AN integral part of our being; it produces one of the strongest drives we experience. In recognition of this fact, the Enemy has filled society with every perversion and depravity imaginable.

From an early age, our children are indoctrinated to perceive as acceptable the very things God calls abominations. This message comes from the media, the educational system, and yes, even the government.

We must be on our guard to censor the things our young children watch, read, listen to, say, and do. We must not be afraid to stand for godly principles in spite of what society calls the "norm."

Holiness means being entirely separated and devoted to God and His work. It signifies purity and commitment to God. Holiness is a command, not an option (1 Peter 1:16).

Prayer

Dear Father, thank You for creating sex as a beautiful thing within the marriage relationship.

I pray that (child's name) will not have any irrational fears about his or her body or sexuality. I pray that he or she will not have an excessive fascination with sexuality.

Lord, please help (child's name) to see himself or herself as fearfully and wonderfully made (Ps. 139:14). Please prevent (child's name) from entertaining the lie of the Devil that he or she ought to be a different gender.

Help (child's name) to be fully committed to a life of holiness and purity. Teach (child's name) to set and enforce boundaries in his or her relationships and to know when to run from a situation or terminate a relationship.

Lord, deliver (child's name) from any sexual phobias or repressions and from any sexual perversion and unclean thoughts or imaginations.

Protect (child's name) from any sexual abuse, assault, or molestation. Please deliver him or her from any deliberate attempt to make him or her sin.

Your Word says You created people male and female; deliver (child's name) from temptation to pursue homosexuality or lesbianism, which are abominations to You (Gen. 1:28; Rom. 1:24–28).

Burgeoning Sexuality

I pray that (child's name) will neither participate in premarital sex nor engage in sex with any one apart from his or her spouse. May (child's name) resist fornication as well as emotional and physical adultery.

If he or she has fallen into any sexual sin, I pray that (child's name) will confess it and receive Your forgiveness and cleansing. Empower him or her to live a life of sexual purity, starting now.

Confessions

The statutes of the Lord are right, bringing joy to (child's name)'s heart, and the commandment of the Lord is pure, enlightening his or her eyes.
—Ps. 19:8

(Child's name) has clean hands and a pure heart; therefore, he or she ascends into the hill of the Lord and stands in His holy place.
—Ps. 24:3–4

(Child's name) runs from fornication to avoid sinning against his or her body.
—1 Cor. 6:18

The light and truth of the Lord lead (child's name).
—Ps. 43:3

Heritage of the Lord

Every word of God is pure. He shields (child's name) from every sexual impurity and trap.
—Prov. 30:5

(Child's name) is good and full of the Holy Ghost, faith, and joy.
—Acts 11:24; 13:52

(Child's name)'s body is the temple of the Holy Ghost, and the Lord will destroy anyone who tries to defile it.
—1 Cor. 3:17; 6:19

The Lord chose (child's name) in Jesus before the foundation of the world, so he or she should be holy and without blame before Him in love.
—Eph. 1:4

(Child's name)'s thoughts are true, honest, just, pure, lovely, of good report, of life, and of praise.
—Phil. 4:8

Jesus has reconciled (child's name) through His death to present him or her holy, blameless, and above reproach in His sight because (child's name) is grounded and settled in the faith.
—Col. 1:22–23

Burgeoning Sexuality

(Child's name) runs away from youthful lusts but follows righteousness, faith, charity, and peace, with them who call on the Lord out of a pure heart.
—2 Tim. 2:22

As an obedient child, (child's name) lives a holy lifestyle even as the Lord is holy.
—1 Peter 1:14–16

(Child's name) was bought with a price; therefore, (child's name) glorifies God in his or her body and spirit, which are God's.
—1 Cor. 6:20

(Child's name) keeps under his or her body and brings it into subjection so as not to be disqualified.
—1 Cor. 9:27

Chapter 12

Leaving and Cleaving

IT IS NEVER too early to start praying about your child's marriage. Next to salvation, the second most important decision in his or her life is the issue of marriage.

A spouse can either make or break someone, and your child must not leave the choice to chance or emotions. Emotions are fickle, and as a believer your child must be "led by the Spirit of God" (Rom. 8:14).

God hates divorce, not the divorced. He forgives divorce just as He forgives any other sin, but divorce takes a toll on all involved—spouses, children, in-laws, and friends. And let us not forget all the financial, material, and custody issues.

If your child is already married, pray that the love of God and unity will be the bedrock of his or her union. Pray that your child and spouse will remove every root of bitterness and pull down every wall of partition. Pray for a teachable, forgiving spirit in the marriage, and that the joy of the Lord would permeate the home.

If your child is at the point of divorce, pray for God to intervene in the matter. Ask God for humility for both parties and that they would hear and do His instructions. Jesus is the resurrection and the life. Pray for restoration and renewal. Pray that both parties would pull up every root of bitterness.

Prayer

> Dear Father, thank You for Your plans to prosper and bless (child's name). Teach (child's name) in the way You have chosen for him or her to go.
>
> (Child's name) is here on Your assignment, and You know who will best encourage, inspire, support, and empower him or her to maximize every grace and excel in his or her calling. I ask that You would help (child's name) to choose a spouse based on Your leading and not primarily because of desire.
>
> I pray that (child's name) will neither become attracted to nor marry either an unbeliever or a believer who is not fully committed to You. If such an attraction already exists, I ask that You would empower (child's name) to break off every soul tie.
>
> I pray that (child's name)'s spouse will be at peace with other family members.

Leaving and Cleaving

I pray that (child's name) will have favor with all his or her in-laws.

I pray that (child's name)'s marriage will be one of love, joy, peace, and fulfillment.

I pray that (child's name)'s marriage will produce strong and healthy male and female children.

I pray that unity and oneness will reign in the home and that each spouse will prefer the other in love.

I pray for restoration in every area of the marriage.

Confessions

(Child's name)'s marriage is honorable in all, and his or her marriage bed is undefiled.
—Heb. 13:4

(Child's name) shall not commit adultery.
—Ex. 20:14

(Child's name) shall not look at anyone with lust.
—Matt. 5:28

(Child's name) and his or her spouse fulfill each other's sexual needs.
—1 Cor. 7:3

My daughter is submissive to her husband so that even if he disobeys the Word of God, without her getting into strife or starting a fight, he will be won by her godly attitude.

—Eph. 5:33

My son loves his wife even as Christ also loved the church and gave Himself for it.

—Eph. 5:25

My son lives with his wife with understanding, giving honor unto her as the weaker vessel and as being heirs together of the grace of life so their prayers are not hindered.

—1 Peter 3:7

Chapter 13

Loving to Learn

IT TAKES HUMILITY to learn. One must acknowledge the fact that he or she is not the source of all knowledge and wisdom. We need to pray that our children will not walk in pride but will possess a teachable, peaceful attitude.

The fear of the Lord is the beginning of wisdom (Ps. 111:10). We must teach our children to have a deep reverence for God and His Word.

No matter the diagnosis or prognosis concerning your child's learning or cognitive abilities, declare what the Word of God says, expecting his or her mind (part of the soul) and brain (physical organ) to conform to God's Word.

Prayer

Thank You, Lord, for giving (child's name) the ability to learn. I pray that (child's name) will be humble and receive instruction and that he or she will possess a quick understanding of concepts and a retentive memory.

I pray that (child's name) will have a deep reverence for You and Your Word at all times. May Your Word be a lamp unto (child's name)'s feet and a light unto his or her path.

Confessions

The Spirit of the Lord rests on (child's name), the Spirit of wisdom and understanding, the Spirit of counsel and might, the Spirit of knowledge and the fear of the Lord. (Child's name) is quick to understand. (Child's name) loves obeying the Lord and will not make rash judgments based on what he or she sees or hears.

—Isa. 11:2–3

The Lord gives (child's name) a spirit of intelligence and understanding.

—Job 32:8

The Lord teaches (child's name), and he or she has great peace.

—Isa. 54:13

Loving to Learn

(Child's name) has more understanding than his or her teachers because he or she meditates on God's Word.
—Ps. 119:99

(Child's name) receives guidance and increases in learning.
—Prov. 1:5

(Child's name) is strong, healthy, good-looking, skillful in all wisdom, and cunning in knowledge. He or she understands science, is fit for promotion, and is teachable.
—Dan. 1:4

The Lord gives (child's name) knowledge and skill in all learning and wisdom so he or she is ten times better than his or her peers.
—Dan. 1:17, 20

Chapter 14

Walking in Healing and Wholeness

IN THE BEGINNING God created everything good. Adam and Eve were created whole—nothing was missing, broken, deformed, or deficient. When they sinned, death came into the earth, and with death came sickness and disease.

Jesus came to save us from sin and its effects by becoming our substitute and paying the penalty for our disobedience. He has acquired for us a rich, full, healthy life.

God anointed Jesus with the Holy Ghost and with power to do good and heal all oppressed by the Devil (Acts 10:38). Sickness is of the Devil, but God is the healer. Throughout Jesus's earthly ministry, He taught and preached the Word and healed every sickness and disease.

Heritage of the Lord

Prayer

Dear Father, thank You for salvation that covers all facets of our lives, including our minds and bodies. Thank You for sending Your Word to heal (child's name) and deliver him or her from all destruction. I praise You that Your Word is medicine to all his or her flesh.

Whatever I permit on earth is permitted in heaven, and whatever I forbid on earth is forbidden in heaven. I forbid any sickness and disease the right to exist in (child's name), and I speak life and wholeness to every DNA, chromosome, cell, tissue, organ, and system.

I uproot everything my Father has not planted and demand that (child's name)'s mind and body conform to the will of God, which is healing and wholeness.

Confessions

(Child's name) serves the Lord, and He blesses his or her bread and water. He also takes sickness away from him or her.

—Ex. 23:25

(Child's name) trusts in the Lord will all his or her heart and does not rely on his or her understanding. (Child's name) acknowledges God in all his or her ways, and He directs his or her path. (Child's name) fears the Lord and departs from evil. This is health to his or her body and strength to his or her bones.

—Prov. 3:5–8

Walking in Healing and Wholeness

(Child's name) pays attention to God's words, keeping them before his or her eyes and in his or her heart, for they are life and healing to all his or her body.
—Prov. 4:20–22

(Child's name)'s merry heart is good medicine.
—Prov. 17:22

The stripes of Jesus have healed (child's name).
—1 Peter 2:24

God's Spirit Who raised Jesus from the dead lives in (child's name); therefore, God makes alive his or her physical body through His Spirit from within.
—Rom. 8:11

I declare that Jesus was wounded for (child's name)'s transgressions and bruised for his or her iniquities: the chastisement of (child name)'s peace was upon Him; and by His stripes he or she is healed.
—Isa. 53:5

The Lord will restore (child's name)'s health, healing all wounds and curing all infections, because there is no hope anywhere else.
—Jer. 30:17

Chapter 15

Taking Proper Care of the Body

STRESS AND FATIGUE, poor eating habits, and a sedentary lifestyle cause or aggravate a lot of diseases. Obesity is fast becoming prevalent in society, even among little children.

God expects our children to take good care of their bodies. It is His temple, and He feels strongly about anything defiling it.

Our children have an assignment to fulfill, and this requires a strong and healthy body. Rest, exercise, and a healthy diet are paramount to enjoying a long, healthy life.

Pray that your children will enjoy good, wholesome food and drink, exercise, and adequate rest.

Prayer

Dear Father, thank You for creating the human body to repair and heal itself. Help (child's name) make right decisions concerning the proper care and feeding of his or her body.

I ask that (child's name) will glorify You in his or her eating and drinking (1 Cor. 10:31) and that he or she will not be gluttonous but keep his or her body under subjection.

Deliver (child's name) from every eating disorder or uncontrollable cravings. Give him or her a desire for wholesome food and exercise, and help (child's name) to take time out for adequate rest.

Deliver (child's name) from every compulsive behavior, such as excessive exercise or weight loss, bulimia, anorexia, poor body image, and self-hatred. Help (child's name) love himself or herself enough to see past how he or she looks on the outside, yet too much to remain unfit.

Confessions

(Child's name) is delivered from every food addiction.

—1 Cor. 6:12

(Child's name) glorifies God in his or her eating and drinking.

—1 Cor. 10:31

Taking Proper Care of the Body

(Child's name) is wise and neither a drunkard nor a glutton.
—Prov. 23:19-21

(Child's name) will both lie down in peace and sleep, for the Lord causes him or her to live in safety.
—Ps. 4:8

(Child's name) goes to bed without being afraid and enjoys sweet, sound sleep.
—Prov. 3:24

Chapter 16

Living in the Place of Protection

THE SAFEST PLACE on earth is in the center of God's will. There is nothing like knowing you are where He has sent you and doing what He has told you to do. No devil in hell can kill you there because you are kept by God. Psalm 91:11 assures us that God has assigned angels to protect and defend us in our ways of service and obedience.

We need to pray that our children will be willing and obedient so they will partake in the best God has for them, including protection and safety.

Prayer

>Dear Father, thank You for watching over (child's name). I pray that he or she will be willing and obedient at all times to ensure continual protection.

Heritage of the Lord

May (child's name) always yield to the leading of Your Spirit, for You will always warn of impending danger.

Preserve (child's name)'s whole being: spirit, soul, and body.

As the mountains surround Jerusalem, so You surround (child's name); as Mount Zion rises in the midst of Jerusalem, he or she shall not be moved.

Be a shield round about (child's name) and keep him or her from every evil oppression.

I ask for preservation from accidents, outbreaks of disease or infection, harm, or any spiritual, physical, mental, or emotional abuse or anguish.

Confessions

(Child's name) will both lie down in peace and sleep, for the Lord causes him or her to live in safety.

—Ps. 4:8

(Child's name) is safe and free from fear of evil because he or she listens to and obeys the Lord.
—Prov. 1:33

(Child's name) is safe, and his or her foot shall not stumble. When (child's name) lies down, he or she shalt not be afraid. He or she shall lie down and have sound sleep.

—Prov. 3:23–24

Living in the Place of Protection

(Child's name) is neither afraid of sudden fear nor of the desolation of the wicked when it comes, for the Lord is his or her confidence and shall keep his or her foot from being taken.
—Prov. 3:25–26

The name of the Lord is a strong tower. (Child's name) runs into it and is safe.
—Prov. 18:10

The fear of man brings a snare, but (child's name) puts his or her trust in the Lord and is safe.
—Prov. 29:25

(Child's name) lives in God's place of protection and under His covering. (Child's name) declares that God is his or her hiding place and trustworthy, reliable defense.

Of a certainty without fail God delivers (child's name) from every trap and outbreak of disease.
—Ps. 91:1–4

(Child's name) will not be afraid of terrorists, weapons, diseases, or disasters because the Lord is a shield round about him or her. These things destroy thousands and tens of thousands around (child's name) but cannot touch him or her.
—Ps. 91:5–7

(Child's name) makes the Lord his or her hiding place and residence; therefore, no evil or calamity overcomes him or her, nor does any disease outbreak come near his or her home.

—Ps. 91:9–10

God has commanded His angels to protect and provide for (child's name) in all his or her ways. (Child's name) tramples upon and crushes every obstacle and weapon the Enemy puts along his or her path of obedience.

—Ps. 91:11–13

(Child's name) loves and trusts in the Lord; therefore He delivers and preserves him or her. The Lord answers and delivers (child's name) from trouble and satisfies him or her with a long and fruitful life.

—Ps. 91:14–16

Chapter 17

Giving Thanks

"O GIVE THANKS UNTO the Lord; for he is good: because his mercy endureth for ever" (Ps. 118:1).

We must thank God for giving us children. It is by His goodness that we have these children, whether by marriage, adoption, foster parenting, or a group home setting. God has entrusted them to us because He expects us to be like Abraham and teach and direct our children to live the way He wants them to.

We must also thank God both for the good we currently see in our children and for that we are yet to see.

Faith expects and calls things into being. We must begin to rejoice in what we hope to see, no matter how contrary things might look right now.

Thanksgiving shows humility. It is an acknowledgment of help received from someone else. When we thank God concerning our children, we admit that it is only by His mercy and grace that we can be effective parents.

Prayer

Dear Father, thank You for the gift of (child's name). I am grateful for the honor and privilege of teaching and commanding him or her in the way You want him or her to go.

I thank You for giving (child's name) life, for being a shield round about him and her and the glory and lifter up of his or her head.

I thank You for all the things I am believing to see in (child's name)'s life. I thank You that (child's name) will love You with all his or her heart, soul, mind, and strength.

I thank You that (child's name) will seek first Your kingdom and Your righteousness so You will provide everything he or she needs.

Thank You for the performance of every promise You have made concerning (child's name).

Confessions

I give thanks to the Lord, for He is good and His mercy toward me and (child's name) is forever.
—Ps. 118:1

Giving Thanks

I give thanks to God that neither will I be forsaken nor will (child's name) beg to eat.
—Ps. 37:25

I thank God that (child's name) will live in His presence and be established before Him.
—Ps. 102:28

I thank God that from everlasting to everlasting His love is with (child's name) and His righteousness with his or her children.
—Ps. 103:17

I thank God that He loves (child's name) and chose him or her to be saved by His Spirit and faith in the truth.
—2 Thess. 2:13

I thank God for making (child's name) fit to share in the inheritance of the saints in light.
—Col. 1:12

I thank God for giving (child's name) the victory through our Lord Jesus Christ.
—1 Cor. 15:57

Heritage of the Lord

I thank God for leading (child's name) in triumph and through him or her spreading the fragrance of His knowledge.

—2 Cor. 2:14

Prayer of Salvation

GOD, I ACKNOWLEDGE the fact that I am a sinner, and come to receive Your gift of eternal life. I confess Jesus as my Lord and Savior and believe in my heart that He died in my place and that You raised Him from the dead.

Thank You, Father, for making me a new being. Old things are gone; all things are new. I am now Your child, and in You I have a future and a hope in Jesus's name. Amen.

To order additional copies of this book call:
1-877-421-READ (7323)
or please visit our website at
www.WinePressbooks.com

If you enjoyed this quality custom-published book,
drop by our website for more books and information.

www.winepresspublishing.com
"Your partner in custom publishing."

CPSIA information can be obtained at www.ICGtesting.com
Printed in the USA
BVOW052328111111

275919BV00004B/1/P